Letting Go of the Chaos

Letting Go *of the* Chaos

Ideas for Addressing Ministry-Related Stress

Victoria Shepp

Saint Mary's Press®

The publishing team included Laurie Delgatto, development editor; Lorraine Kilmartin, reviewer; prepress and manufacturing coordinated by the production departments of Saint Mary's Press.

Copyright © 2007 by Saint Mary's Press, Christian Brothers Publications, 702 Terrace Heights, Winona, MN 55987-1318, www.smp.org. All rights reserved. No part of this book may be reproduced by any means without the written permission of the publisher.

Printed in the United States of America

3828

ISBN 978-0-88489-953-2

Library of Congress Cataloging-in-Publication Data

Shepp, Victoria.
    Letting go of the chaos : ideas for addressing ministry-related stress / Victoria Shepp.
    p. cm.
  ISBN 978-0-88489-953-2 (pbk.)
    1. Church youth workers—Job stress—Prayers and devotions. 2. Church work with youth—Catholic Church—Prayers and devotions. I. Title.

BX2347.8.Y7S54 2007
248.8'9—dc22

2006103009

Author Acknowledgments

I would like to thank a few people who made this book possible. First, I thank Laurie Delgatto, my editor and friend, who brought the idea for this book to me, let me play with the idea, and worked with me to create the final version.

Second, I want to thank Paulette, the person who helps me de-stress and who reads every word I write and challenges me to be the best minister I can be. I hope all people in ministry have someone like her to turn to.

Finally, I want to thank the youth ministry leaders who have sat around the table with me throughout the years—those who have helped me with my stress, those who have trusted me with their own stressful times, and those who identified the stressors addressed in this book. These leaders are why I wrote this book. They live and work "in the trenches," and it is my hope that they will continue to do the great work they do, maybe with a little help from this guide.

Contents

Introduction 8

Section 1: Emotional Stress

1. Dealing with Others' Problems 12
2. Balancing Family, Friends, and Ministry. 14
3. Staying "Adult" While Working with Youth 16
4. Being Mindful of Gender Issues. 18
5. Being Too Young (or Too Old) for Ministry 20

Section 2: Physical Stress

6. Living with Crazy Schedules That Wreak Havoc on Sleep 24
7. Living with Crazy Schedules That Wreak Havoc on Exercise Routine. 26
8. Living with Crazy Schedules That Wreak Havoc on Diets 28
9. Having Difficulties Keeping Up with Youth . . . 30
10. Doing Real Physical Work. 32

Section 3: Intellectual Stress

11. Keeping Things Age Appropriate 36
12. Thinking You Need to Have All the Answers . . . 38
13. Keeping Up with Church Documents 40
14. Coming from Another Faith Tradition or Coming Back After Leaving the Church 42
15. Seeking Out Ongoing Training and Formation . . . 44

Section 4: Spiritual Stress

16. Living Up to the Call of Ministry 48
17. Living Up to a Certain Spiritual Standard 50
18. Staying Humble 52
19. Dealing with Times of Spiritual Dryness 54
20. Taking Time for Prayer 56

Acknowledgments 59

Introduction

Did you know that an online search using the key word *stress* generates about 290,000,000 results? We all know that too much stress can seriously affect our physical, mental, intellectual, and spiritual well-being. Simply put, stress affects all of us each and every day. We experience stress in our work, in our family lives, and, yes, even (or maybe mostly) in our faith lives. This is especially true for those of us who serve in ministry with the young.

Working with young people can be invigorating and joyful, but it can also be tiring and stressful. Too often those of us in ministry put aside our own needs for those of the young people we serve. We can forget the importance of finding time to renew our own minds, bodies, and spirits so we can continue to effectively minister to others. That's why we should always strive to control our stress before it controls us. The time and energy we spend managing stress will pay off in the long run by promoting health, happiness, and holiness in our lives.

How This Book Came to Be

A few years ago, I presented a workshop on creating balance in ministry. It revealed some of the stresses that many of us in ministry face. Two years after the workshop began, an idea for this book came about. In preparation for writing this book, I invited ministry leaders (volunteer and paid) to join me for what became a lengthy conversation about the stresses that so many of us face in the everyday happenings of ministry to and with young people. That gathering offered some great insights about ministry and stress, including what I consider four distinct areas in which stress and ministry overlap: emotional, physical, intellectual, and spiritual. These areas became the focus for this book.

How to Use This Book

The book is divided into four sections, each addressing one of the four areas mentioned above. Each chapter begins with a story or words of wisdom drawn from the Scriptures or a writing by a saint or modern-day Church leader. A short reflection follows to help you explore more fully the topic at hand. Each chapter also offers some questions for your consideration. You may either silently reflect on those questions, journal about them, or find someone to share your responses with. Each chapter also provides practical considerations and ways for you to work toward addressing (and hopefully conquering) the stress. These are simple, easy-to-achieve ideas. Finally, each chapter concludes with a simple prayer as a means for you to connect with God and ask for guidance in dealing with the stress in your ministry life.

You might consider reading the book from start to finish, or you might decide to come back to the book when a certain type of stress begins creeping into your life. How you choose to use the book's content is completely up to you.

Some Closing Thoughts

If you are like many youth ministry leaders (including me), you too have stress. I hope you can see past the stress and use the practical suggestions within this book to move beyond it. I don't guarantee a stress-free ministry, but I do hope this book helps you live beyond the chaos.

—Vikki Shepp

Section 1
Emotional Stress

1
Dealing with Others' Problems

Our Story

> Come to me, all you that are weary and are carrying heavy burdens, and I will give you rest. Take my yoke upon you. . . . For my yoke is easy, and my burden is light.
>
> (Matthew 11:28–30)

Reflection

The Gospel of Matthew gives insight into what Jesus wants us to do when we face problems and difficult times. First, we must place our concerns before God, knowing that God always provides the guidance we need to get through anything. The Gospel also tells us that we are called to be Jesus to others and to help bring about hope and healing. This is what we do when we practice good pastoral care. Effective pastoral care does not mean, however, that we are to take on or handle everyone else's problems. Good pastoral care is about listening well, helping youth and their families find appropriate resources for guidance and counseling, and providing opportunities for young people to reach out to help and support one another. Effective pastoral care also means that those of us in ministry must acknowledge that we may not always have the training, skills, experience, or expertise to help the young people or families we know and serve, especially those who are dealing with serious problems or crises. Trying to take on problems we are not equipped to handle will invariably create havoc and stress not only for us but also for the people we are trying to help. This means we must see our limitations and direct young people and families to the right people for necessary support and guidance.

Questions to Ponder

- What is my understanding of the youth ministry component of pastoral care?
- Do I have a pastoral care plan (one that has phone numbers and contact information) that I can use when a young person or parent needs help? If not, what will it take for me to create one?
- Who is a safe person I can go to (confidentially) when I need to process someone else's problem?

For Consideration

- Create a pastoral care resource plan and contact list. Include the pastor's emergency pager number or cell phone number, as well as contact information for counselors for drug or suicide issues and for other agencies that you can refer youth and their families to in times of crisis.
- Know your limits! If you are not a trained counselor, be sure of what issues you are unable or untrained to handle. Know when to refer a young person or family to the experts.
- Remember that prayer is an essential element in any pastoral care effort. Take the time to pray for those young people and families who are dealing with tough times.

Prayer

God of compassion and understanding, guide me as I provide healthy pastoral care to the young people and families I serve. Help me remember the importance of taking care of myself as well. May I mirror your qualities of compassion and understanding by listening with my heart and helping with my mind. Amen.

2

Balancing Family, Friends, and Ministry

Our Story

Oh how important is discipline, community, prayer, silence, caring presence, simple listening, adoration, and deep, lasting faithful friendship. We all want it so much, and still the powers suggesting that all of that is fantasy are enormous. But we have to replace the battle for power with the battle to create space for the spirit.

(Henri Nouwen)

Reflection

How many times do we say, "I need to make time to go to lunch with my friends," or "I should really take a weekend off to visit my folks," but never end up making the time to do so? Maintaining a balanced life includes creating the necessary time to spend with the people we care about. Too many of us carry around a "ministry mentality" that tells us we have to be present for every meeting, every class, and every ministry function on the calendar. This is a false mentality! Even Jesus took time away from the people he served to be with his closest friends.

It is important to realize that we become less effective, less pastoral, less whole, and more stressed when we don't balance our ministerial life with our personal life. Just as you would schedule a retreat for youth or a community-building activity, schedule time to spend with your family and friends.

Questions to Ponder

- When was the last time I had a casual lunch or dinner with friends (not colleagues)?
- How much of my calendar includes time that is planned as family time or friend time?
- How can I create better balance among my time for ministry, time for my family and friends, and time for myself?

For Consideration

- Color-code your appointment book or calendar. Use a different color for work and fun. See if your time is in balance week by week.
- Make a date with yourself. Block the time on your appointment book or calendar as "Very Important Appointment," and keep your date with yourself!
- Prepay for an event that is just for you and your significant other (or best friend). If it is prepaid, you'll be less likely to cancel.

Prayer

Father, Son and Holy Spirit, in your Triune nature, you show me the importance of community, family, and friends. I turn to you to help guide me in keeping my family and friends in balance with my ministry. As I spend time with my family and friends, be with all of us and inspire us to be like you—a community of love. Amen.

3

Staying "Adult" While Working with Youth

Our Story

Do you have a faith that is such that it is able to touch the hearts of your students and inspire them with the Christian spirit? This is the greatest miracle you could perform and the one that God asks of you, for this is the purpose of your work.

(Saint John Baptist de La Salle)

Reflection

"That is so *groovy!*"
"That is so awesomely *cool!*"
"That is so totally *bad!*"
"That is so majorly *phat!*"

No matter what decade it is, young people have sayings to let us know what is in (or out) of style. Though knowing what is "in" or "out" is important to those of us who work with youth, trying to be in style may not be and can often add undue stress to our lives. Though it is important that we understand youth culture, we must also remain in the adult world.

If you are spending all your time with teenagers and know more about the world they live in than you do about the adult world, then it's time to schedule some adult time. Be sure to include such time in your schedule, including time for exercise and time for family. If you don't schedule it, it is easy to postpone. Adult time is important, as it gives a different perspective (a grown-up one) and helps us stay in touch with the realities of the world.

Remember that good youth ministry is about touching the hearts of young people. It is not about being cool.

Questions to Ponder

- How do I distinguish myself from the young people I work with?
- How do young people know I am there for them but not "one of them"?
- What are some other ways I can stay "adult"?

For Consideration

- Spend adequate time with adults by scheduling time with your peers in ministry, with your friends, and with your adult family members.
- Do keep up on the latest pop culture, but maintain professionalism and an adult perspective in your work.
- Being the adult in youth ministry also means dressing the part. This is not to say you can't be fashionable; it just means the young people don't need to see you *look* like them. They just need you to like (and accept) them.

Prayer

Ageless and timeless God, help me to stay adult while working with young people. May I be an example of your love and compassion, not of the trends and styles of the times. As I spend time with young people, help me to be immersed in the moment without losing my perspective. I thank you for the gifts young people bring to me, and I pray that I am a gift to them as well. Amen.

4

Being Mindful of Gender Issues

Our Story

Saint Francis of Assisi and Saint Clare had a rich friendship based on a love of Christ and mutual values. Although their friendship took place in the thirteenth century, it is an example of the importance of being mindful of the other gender. Saint Francis held Saint Clare and all the Poor Ladies (he never called them nuns or sisters) in esteem. Saint Clare based her order on Francis's. These two give witness to the importance of collaboration and respect among men and women.

Reflection

It is likely that at some point in our lives, each of us has been in a situation that made us feel "less than," or inferior. We all know that not feeling good enough can cause us to doubt ourselves, which in turn can result in feeling stressed out. This is especially true when dealing with issues of gender. Messages in the media too often tell us what we can and cannot do because of our gender. Scores of cartoons, sitcoms, and stand-up routines are based on the differences between the sexes. There are books—scientific, anecdotal, and humorous—that teach us about the other gender.

    We know that language plays a central role in the ways we behave and think. The language we use provides an important model for the young people and community we serve. Not being sensitive to gender needs can land us in some uncomfortable and stressful situations. When planning programs, events, and other activities, or even when having conversations, we must remember that word choices often reflect unconscious assumptions about gender roles. As ministry leaders, we need to examine any language that may silence, stereotype, or constrain others. If we do not, we will end up dealing with the effects of not being inclusive of all.

Questions to Ponder

- How do I consider the perspectives of both genders when planning my programming?
- In what ways do I recognize the gifts of my own gender?
- How do I present a balanced view of the other gender when working with young people?

For Consideration

- Imagine what your life would be like if you were born as the opposite gender. Consider how your life might be different.
- List all the stereotypes you can (positive and negative) about the opposite gender. Then ask yourself if you reflect those stereotypes in your actions or words.
- Speak up when you hear others speaking badly of either gender. When you are the focus of such bias, tell the other person (or persons) how such comments make you feel.

Prayer

Father and Mother God, you made us, male and female, in your image. Be with me as I minister with and to those who are the same gender as me as well as with and to those of the opposite gender. When I become insensitive of the other gender, gently remind me that we are created equally, wonderfully, and beautifully in your image. Amen.

5
Being Too Young (or Too Old) for Ministry

Our Story

In the Scriptures, we are told that Sarah felt old and tired, while Timothy felt young and incapable. Both felt their age was an impediment. Yet Sarah, at the age of ninety, became mother to Isaac, who gave rise to nations and rulers of peoples (see Genesis 17:16)! And Timothy became the first youth leader of the New Testament.

Reflection

Throughout the Old and New Testaments, we find accounts of God's calling men and woman of various ages. God does not call us based on our age but rather on our talents, our passions, our hearts, and our willingness to serve. However, sometimes each of us struggles with how our age may affect the good work we strive to do. Whether you are feeling too young or too old, you need to recognize the gift of your current age. Consider making a list of the benefits of your age (for example, "I am twenty and am aware of trends" or "I am fifty and helped my own kids through adolescence"). Knowing the downfalls of one's age is equally important. For example, at a certain age, most youth ministry leaders stop trying to be trendy. (Very few forty-five-year-olds look good in teen fash-ions anyway!)

Age (too much or too little) does not disqualify anyone from serving the young. But it takes work to stick it out for the long haul. If ministry isn't enjoyable or life-giving to you anymore, then it may be time to re-evaluate whether you should continue to serve in this capacity.

Questions to Ponder

- When do I try to act like a teenager just to get young people to like me?
- In what ways am I remembering to be childlike and not childish (or teenlike but not teenish)?
- How do I try to understand teen culture without having to live in it?

For Consideration

- Think about all the things that drew you to ministry with young people. Then spend some time reflecting on whether those things still apply to you today.
- Make a list of your gifts that connect to your particular age or stage. Embrace those gifts.
- If you feel your age is negatively affecting your ministry, seek out a colleague, your pastor, or a ministry friend and talk about how you might work to address your concerns. Some simple training or skill building may be just what you need to work through the challenges and stressors.

Prayer

Creator God, who called Timothy at a young age and who blessed Sarah in her old age, let me live by the example that each set for me. May I be the kind of minister that both young and old turn to. Thank you for this opportunity that has come in this stage in my life. Amen.

Section 2
Physical Stress

6
Living with Crazy Schedules That Wreak Havoc on Sleep

Our Story

I lie down and sleep;
I wake again, for the Lord sustains me.

(Psalm 3:5)

Reflection

Sleep is a natural part of everyone's life, but many of us know little about how important it is. Sleep is something our bodies need to do; it is not an option. Sleep does indeed sustain us. Not only does it regenerate our physical being, but it also allows us to shut down and regenerate our brain. Not having enough sleep lowers performance and concentration.

Unfortunately, youth ministry often can include many late-night meetings, early-morning staff days, and long weekends, which often equate to missed opportunities for good sleep. How often do we exchange a good night's sleep for a few extra hours to complete our to-do list? Although missing a full night's sleep once in a while is okay (though not recommended), a consistent lack of good sleep is hard on the body, mind, and spirit. In order to be fully present to the young people we serve, we need regular restful sleep.

If adequate rest is not a part of your daily routine, then it is time to evaluate your schedule and make adjustments.

Questions to Ponder

- How do I try to compensate for lack of sleep?
- What do I do when I have the opportunity to go to bed early?
- When I need sleep, how do I plan for a good night's rest?

For Consideration

- Schedule, schedule, schedule! Be sure to schedule smart. If you are planning to attend a late-night event, plan a later start the next day, if possible.
- Catnaps (about 20 minutes long) are a great way to rev up your energy—without the side effects of caffeine.
- Learn to recognize your own body's language. Dark circles and sallow skin are a few signs of lack of sleep.

Prayer

God who invented the yawn and the art of sleeping in, help me take care of my body, mind, and spirit through proper sleeping habits. And help me on those days when I haven't had enough sleep. Fill me with the energy of the Holy Spirit so I can get my work done. Amen.

7
Living with Crazy Schedules That Wreak Havoc on Exercise Routine

Our Story

Before his illness made it too difficult, Pope John Paul II made a point to include physical activity in his regular schedule. Some of the most popular photographs of his early religious life and papacy include pictures of him skiing and hiking. Even in his later years, he made time to hike in his beloved hills. Through these actions, he offered an example of the value of getting fresh air, exercise, and physical renewal.

Reflection

In New Testament times, the disciples didn't have to worry about saturated fat or making it to the gym on time; eating naturally and getting plenty of exercise was part of everyday life. Walking from town to town gave them plenty of exercise and fresh air. Unfortunately, we modern-day disciples have numerous distractions that often get in the way of taking time to exercise. This often leads to our making excuses for not exercising and properly taking care of our physical selves. Yet the Scriptures tell us that the body is the "temple of the Holy Spirit" (1 Corinthians 6:19), and the New Testament instructs us to take care of the body.

Such care includes taking time to exercise. If a formal routine or a structured workout is really out of the question for you, there are numerous DVDs and magazines that offer ideas for simple exercises you can do at home or at your desk or office with simple objects like soup cans and water bottles. Comprehensive youth ministry focuses on building up the whole person, which includes the body, so get out of your seat and on your feet!

Questions to Ponder

- What is my exercise routine? If I don't have one now, what was it before I became involved in ministry?
- What type of exercise do I enjoy, and how might I incorporate it into my daily or weekly schedule?
- What are the motivating factors for exercising?

For Consideration

- Some medical insurance plans offer reimbursement for health club memberships. See if yours does. If so, take advantage of it.
- If joining a gym or health club is out of the question, get creative. If you know a few other people who are in need of an exercise routine, gather them together and form a walking club, or set up a schedule for various types of exercise for the group.
- Contribute to your overall exercise plan by doing little things throughout the day (like sit-ups before your shower, a 20-minute walk after lunch, and arm lifts before bed).

Prayer

God of muscle and bone, God of speed and grace, help me find an exercise routine that works for me. Help me get to the place where moving is fun and freeing and joyful. May I treat this body of mine in the way it deserves, and may I, in the process of caring for my body, realize the graces of the spirit that are exercised at the same time. Amen.

8
Living with Crazy Schedules That Wreak Havoc on Diets

Our Story

> Now John was clothed with camel's hair, with a leather belt around his waist, and he ate locusts and wild honey.
>
> (Mark 1:6)

Reflection

No one expects those of us in ministry to eat locusts and honey (even if we are planning a youth ministry version of *Fear Factor*). And unbeknownst to some, pizza, soda, and snacks are not three of the major food groups.

Part of the problem of not eating well can be attributed to a lack of mindfulness while eating. To solve this dilemma, we really must begin by considering some simple tenets of mindful eating: (1) stop to enjoy what you are eating, (2) eat in quiet and focus on your food, (3) put your fork down in between bites, and (4) let your body tell you when it is full. We must also be mindful of the food choices we make. Though it might seem more convenient to grab a doughnut as a morning meal, we all know that healthy foods (how about a piece of fruit instead?) help fuel our minds and bodies much more adequately.

Good eating habits will help us feel (and look) better as well as reduce stress. Good habits will also set an example for those we minister with and to. And we all know that when we look better, we feel better. So stay away from those doughnuts and grab a shiny apple instead.

Questions to Ponder

- What eating habits do I model for the young people I serve?
- When I plan my meals, how do I consider the other events of the day? For example, if I know that there is going to be an ice cream-making party for the eighth graders, do my breakfast and lunch choices include low-fat and healthy foods?
- When and how do I make time for preparing healthy meals for myself?

For Consideration

- Plan, plan, plan! It takes planning to eat in healthy ways. Get out your calendar and look at the events that include food. Plan your healthy eating around those events if necessary.
- Check out Web sites and cookbooks that cater to busy people. You will find lots of ideas for healthy, fast, and easy eating.
- Provide healthy options for the youth too. For snack breaks, provide fresh fruit, carrot sticks, and other nonprocessed foods.

Prayer

God who provides pizza and broccoli, may I balance my eating of both. I thank you for all the delicious food I have at my disposal. May I always be thankful for what I have, and help me, God of chocolate and soda, to make good choices in what I eat. May I be mindful of, and grateful for, what I eat. Amen.

9
Having Difficulties Keeping Up with Youth

Our Story

God can use our weakness as easily as our strength in order to accomplish his will.

(Pope John Paul II)

Reflection

Those of us in ministry must always remember that we are valued for our love of the faith and for our example of what it means to live a life of discipleship rather than for our ability to win a relay race or keep up with a group of teenagers. Though effective youth ministry often includes community building and other physical activities with young people (no matter how silly those activities might be), that doesn't mean you have to put yourself at risk for physical injury in an attempt to "keep up with the kids." If a particular game is just too physical, stressful, or uncomfortable for you, it is okay to step out. In doing so, you also give example (and permission) to young people who may choose to opt out for similar reasons. We all know that no one should ever be forced to participate in an activity that challenges his or her physical or emotional limitations.

Questions to Ponder

- Why is it important to know your limitations?
- In what ways do you show others that sitting out can be healthy and okay?

- In what ways do you participate while still being mindful of your limitations?

For Consideration

- When planning youth gatherings and events, include a variety of activities that allow for the inclusion of all.
- Make a job description for yourself. Keep the expectations for "keeping up with youth" realistic.
- Don't be afraid to speak up when an activity makes you feel uncomfortable or stressed. Model the need for good and honest communication with the adults and young people you minister to and with.

Prayer

Never-tiring God, thank you for the gifts of young people—for their energy and enthusiasm. Thank you for bringing young people into my life and for helping me stay young at heart. When I am unable to keep up with them, lift me and hold me. Remind me, Lord, that there are times when it is okay to be the observer. I know you'll give me the strength to do what I need to do to be a true spiritual companion to the young people I serve. Amen.

10
Doing Real Physical Work

Our Story

> We can do no great things—only small things with great love. . . . When someone told me that the Sisters had not started any big work, that they were quietly doing small things, I said even if they helped one person, that was enough. Jesus would have died for one person, for one sinner.
>
> (Mother Teresa)

Reflection

It is true that youth ministry often involves a lot of physical work. In addition to carrying heavy items, such as cases of soda and boxes of *The Catholic Youth Bible*®, there are times when setting up (and putting away) tables and chairs can seem to become our sole enterprise. The physical work that comes with youth ministry can be taxing, stressful, and sometimes even dangerous if done alone. The "I can do it myself" model of ministry isn't a good example to the youth or the adults we serve, nor is it good for our physical well-being. Knowing our own limitations is important to the physical work of ministry. Asking for help is not a sign of physical weakness; rather, it is a sign that we recognize our limitations and are not afraid to ask for help when and if we need it.

Mother Teresa knew that by working together with others, the heavy work got done. We too need to remember that the work is always easier when done with others.

Questions to Ponder

- How do I enlist the help of others when doing the heavy work?
- How do I know when to stop doing physical work—how do I listen to my body?
- How do I differentiate between doing regular tasks and real physical work that may harm me?

For Consideration

- Plan loading and unloading, setup and tear-down, while you plan the other parts of events. Give yourself and your team enough time to do the physical work.
- Know your parish or school's policy regarding the maintenance staff. If staff is available, request their assistance when needed.
- Schedule time to take care of yourself. Get a massage or a pedicure (or just take a long soak in a bath) after an intense event requiring physical work.

Prayer

Lord whose physical strength is beyond measure, fill me with your strength to do the work I am called to do, and fill me with your wisdom and humility to know when to ask for help. When I'm tired, refresh me; when I'm sore, soothe me; and when I need rest, let it be with you. Amen.

Section 3
Intellectual Stress

11
Keeping Things Age Appropriate

Our Story

Effective ministry with adolescents provides developmentally appropriate experiences, programs, activities, strategies, resources, content, and processes to address the unique developmental and social needs of young and older adolescents both as individuals and as members of families.

(United States Conference of Catholic Bishops)

Reflection

How many times have you shaken your head in frustration or wanted to scream because the young people you had gathered just didn't "get it" in regard to the topic of discussion or an activity you asked them to complete? One of the greatest stresses we experience in ministry is the young people's not "getting it" or not fully participating, but that is often the result of our not doing our homework in regard to their developmental capabilities. One of the themes of a comprehensive vision for Catholic youth ministry, as put forth by the bishops in *Renewing the Vision* (1997), is age appropriateness. This means meeting young people where they are—sometimes physically, but especially spiritually and developmentally.

Different age-groups reach milestones in each domain at different times. For example, most physical competencies are achieved in the early ages, and most of the basic "hardwiring" of adult logic and thinking skills begin to appear around age twelve. Observing with an open mind the young people we serve allows us to see where their specific needs and strengths lie.

We don't need a doctorate in psychology to minister to young people, but a little background on child development will help us build programs and activities that are more effective and appropriate.

Questions to Ponder

- What is my understanding of the developmental needs of young people (and adults)?
- How do I currently address the developmental needs I encounter in youth?
- What is my typical response when the young people don't "get it"? Is this an appropriate response? How might I respond differently?

For Consideration

- Read up on the developmental needs of young people.
- Become familiar with the National Study of Youth and Religion. (For the Catholic results, check out the National Federation for Catholic Youth Ministry. For the national results, see *Soul Searching*, by Christian Smith.)
- Periodically check youth ministry programming, lesson plans, and activities to see if they are age and developmentally appropriate.

Prayer

God who walks with me regardless of what stage I am in, lead me to a deeper understanding of the young people I serve. Help me to know them more fully and to be accepting of their developmental needs. May the work I do help them grow, and may I, in doing the work, grow as well. Amen.

12

Thinking You Need to Have All the Answers

Our Story

Happy are those who find wisdom, and those who get understanding.

(Proverbs 3:13)

Reflection

Let's face it—none of us has the answers to every question asked. And don't each of us know how humbling it can be to sit with a group of adolescents who have questions we find ourselves unable to answer? It's even more difficult (and humbling) to have to respond "I don't know" to a question asked by another adult or one of our peers. When we find ourselves in these types of situations, we essentially have two choices: (1) to make up an answer so we look like we know what we're talking about or (2) to simply tell the truth by saying, "I don't know." The latter is a much more humbling and less stressful response, and it's essential to good, honest, and effective ministry. The truth is that we don't have to know every answer to every question. What we do need, however, is a willingness to seek out answers.

Questions to Ponder

- What do I do when I don't know the answer to a question?
- What resources do I have for finding answers?
- How might I encourage young people to seek out their own answers?

For Consideration

- Create a file of references and responses for commonly asked questions about the faith.
- Take time to read up on the areas where you feel unqualified or unprepared.
- If you are too hard on yourself, lighten up! Though it is important to understand Catholic practices and beliefs, you don't have to be a theologian to effectively minister to young people.

Prayer

God of all wisdom, of all answers, and of all knowledge, thank you for what I already know. As I challenge myself to learn more, I trust you will lead me to the answers I seek. Help me to not think I need to know everything, and help me grow in wisdom and in guiding young people to wisdom as well. Amen.

13
Keeping Up with Church Documents

Our Story

Beware the man of one book.

(Saint Thomas Aquinas)

Reflection

Great writings are important to our Tradition. Such great writings include the Bible, the *Catechism of the Catholic Church*, the writings of the saints, and papal encyclicals. Other documents, such as *Renewing the Vision*, the *National Directory for Catechesis*, and the *General Directory for Catechesis*, have been important contributions to the field of ministry with the young. It is imperative that we are aware of, read, and study such writings and documents in order to articulate key Church teachings, practices, and beliefs to the young people we serve. When we don't stay current on important Church documents, we can find ourselves inadequately prepared to teach and stressed out about discussing important matters of faith.

If you have become a person of just one book—even if it is the Bible—you may be missing out on the other rich writings of our Tradition that speak to your role as minister and active member of the Church.

Questions to Ponder

- What great writings and documents do I currently own (or have access to)? Of those, which do I know well and which do I need to read or review?

- Whom can I work with to learn more about helpful Church writings and documents?
- How can I find out which writings and documents are important to my ministry?

For Consideration

- Schedule time in your appointment book or calendar (weekly or monthly) to do some reading. Doing so on a regular basis will help keep you less stressed than having to do a lot of reading at one time.
- One way to keep up with current Church writings and documents is to regularly visit the National Federation for Catholic Youth Ministry Web site and the United States Conference of Catholic Bishops' Web site.
- If your diocesan office provides in-services on new documents, do your best to attend those sessions. This is a simple but effective way to keep up to date.

Prayer

God who spoke through burning bushes and winds of fire, speak to me through the written words of the people of our Church. Help me see the wisdom of those words and the ways they can help me improve my ministry. Amen.

14

Coming from Another Faith Tradition or Coming Back After Leaving the Church

Our Story

> To be a child of God means to go hand-in-hand with God, to do his will, not one's own; to place all our hopes and cares in his hands and no longer be concerned about one's self or future. . . . If this can be done, then one can freely live on for the present and for the future.
>
> (Edith Stein)

Reflection

Converting to Catholicism has its advantages; people who convert do so as a personal choice rather than becoming Catholic through infant Baptism, which of course is something a parent chooses for a child. Often converts receive adult-level formation while their peers may have ended formal religious education in the eighth or ninth grade. This may also be true for adults who were raised Catholic but left the Church and later returned.

I'm a convert; becoming Catholic as a young adult definitely was my own decision. However, I don't "own" some of the collective memories children often gain being raised in the faith. For example, memories of praying the rosary as a family or learning a popular devotion from a favorite grandparent just aren't part of my experience. As a convert, my Catholic identity took a steep learning curve, and I often feel like I've lost out on the gradual, spongelike faith development that "cradle Catholics" experience.

If you are a convert to the faith, or if you have returned to the faith after some time away, don't see that as a deficit; see it as an opportunity to share the faith differently, but still effectively.

Questions to Ponder

- How did I acquire my faith?
- If I am a convert or a returning Catholic, how have I learned or strengthened my understanding of the traditions, practices, and beliefs of the Catholic faith?
- How would someone walking into my home or office know I am Catholic?

For Consideration

- Regardless of your status as a convert, cradle Catholic, or returning Catholic, know what you believe and why you believe it.
- Consider adding some of the Catholic traditions and symbols to your home and office space.
- Have some conversations with people you recognize as having a well-developed faith life. Find out what they do to continue to grow in their faith and understanding of the Church.

Prayer

God who hears all people's prayers, accept mine as a person who chooses the Catholic way of expressing my discipleship to you. Let me recognize the gifts of my faith and of my childhood as precious gifts from you. May my faith journey reflect these gifts and my ministry reflect your will. Amen.

15

Seeking Out Ongoing Training and Formation

Our Story

> Every individual has the responsibility to grow in faith and to contribute to the growth in faith of the other members of the Church.
>
> (United States Conference of Catholic Bishops)

Reflection

Being called to ministry includes a responsibility to be well trained to carry out our ministries effectively. Simply stated, not being properly trained or educated will always result in undue stress and a whole lot of mistakes. None of us would expect a man to say, "I'm called to be a priest," and then the next week see him preside at a Sunday liturgy. We expect him to discern and to go through proper formation, training, direction, and prayer to prepare for ordination. Our role in youth ministry isn't that different. Once called, we too are required to further our knowledge, formation, and skills. This mandate for formation not only comes from Church documents on ministry but is a directive of discipleship. Formation in spirituality, in the Catholic faith, and in the practices of good ministry should always be ongoing. When we seek out opportunities to grow in faith, we find we are better equipped (and less stressed) to meet the needs of the community. The more we know, the more effective we can be.

Questions to Ponder

- Whom do I know that is well informed and formed, and how did he or she get such training?
- What type of additional training do I want or need?
- What areas do I need to revisit to renew my level of competency?

For Consideration

- There are many ways to be formed and informed for ministry. Look into online courses, gathered events, in-services, diocesan events, and conferences.
- Make a list of the types of training you'd like to receive. Refer to the list when you hear about parish, diocesan, regional, and national events. If you are struggling to make time for training, prioritize your list and attend sessions in order of the priorities.
- Utilize Web sites, books, and magazines as training tools.

Prayer

Creator God, you have revealed yourself to me and called me to serve your Church. Continue to show me the areas where I need to continue to grow in knowledge. Give me a willing heart to learn more about you and more about ministry, and let me see how my willing heart reveals you to others. Amen.

Section 4
Spiritual Stress

16
Living Up to the Call of Ministry

Our Story

> What God gives sometimes seems so great . . . and we feel so poor! He offers us what we can scarcely imagine: Christ and the Holy Spirit come to dwell within our hearts irresistibly.
>
> (Brother Roger of Taizé)

Reflection

Sometimes it seems like the more we meditate and pray, the more unworthy we feel. Reading and reflecting on the life of Christ, studying the lives of the saints, and listening to modern-day prophets can be quite humbling. During the times when we find ourselves saying, "Maybe I don't know enough, or am not good enough to serve," we must remember that God needs men and women like you and me to proclaim the Good News of Jesus Christ to the young. Although we might respond to times of unworthiness by saying, "I am just a woman (or man), not a saint or even a very holy person," we must always recognize that Christ dwells within our hearts and that we are called to let others see and experience Christ through us. Because Jesus is no longer physically here on earth, we proclaim him through our words and actions.

Just remember that as long as your ministry to the young honors God, God will be pleased with your effort.

Questions to Ponder

- How do I respond to others when they express thanks for the ministry I offer?

- How do I show others that our baptismal call makes each of us worthy (and responsible) for the work of the Church?
- What kind of self-talk can I initiate when I am feeling overwhelmed, stressed out, or unworthy of my ministry? Whom can I seek out to help me find some clarity and direction?

For Consideration

- Allow yourself to be thanked and given credit for what you do.
- If there is an area in your ministry where you do indeed feel inadequate, gain understanding or get training in that area.
- Make a list of the things you do well. Keep that list and refer to it when you are feeling unworthy.

Prayer

Thank you, Lord, for making me worthy of the call to serve you and others. By your very presence, I am empowered to be in ministry. I know it is up to me to gain experience and knowledge, and I ask for your guidance and support when I feel unworthy of this call. Amen.

17

Living Up to a Certain Spiritual Standard

Our Story

> [After Jesus came to his disciples in the boat,] Peter answered him, "Lord, if it is you, command me to come to you on the water." He said, "Come." So Peter got out of the boat, started walking on the water, and came toward Jesus. But when he noticed the strong wind, he became frightened, and beginning to sink, he cried out, "Lord, save me!" Jesus immediately reached out his hand and caught him, saying to him, "You of little faith, why did you doubt?" When they got into the boat, the wind ceased. And those in the boat worshiped him, saying, "Truly you are the Son of God."
>
> (Matthew 14:28–33)

Reflection

Because we often make mistakes, it is comforting to know that Jesus entrusted the "keys of the Church" to someone who also made mistakes throughout the Gospels. Peter (and his fellow disciples) continually made mistakes. Too often Jesus's followers didn't believe Jesus, so they made him prove things, and they grumbled over his actions and even fell asleep on him. However, many of us (Jesus's modern-day disciples) don't allow ourselves the same margin of error. Being in ministry, some of us believe, requires perfection. But perfection is not what Jesus requires. Jesus requires us to live up to a standard: to love others. Like Peter, we need faith. This can be challenging or stressful when, for example, our own teenager is the one caught with contraband on a retreat, or when a family is going through a difficult time, such as dealing with divorce. Remembering Peter's actions and living his ultimate answer, "Yes, Lord; you know that I love you" (John 21:15), is the standard to strive for.

Questions to Ponder

- What standards have I set for myself?
- How might these standards be unrealistic? How might these standards be causing me stress?
- Who or what helps me keep my standards? Who or what keeps me from achieving my standards?

For Consideration

- Review the standards set by the diocese (or the National Federation for Catholic Youth Ministry) regarding youth ministry. This includes national core competencies in ministry as well as a code of ethics.
- Remember that God does not call us to be perfect; God calls us simply to love others.
- Allow yourself to be human!

Prayer

Peter's friend, and mine too, you are the perfect one, not me. Help me live the way you intend—as a person who strives for holiness rather than perfection. Help me to recognize my strengths and weaknesses and to be open to others who also make mistakes. Guide my decisions and continue to love me the way I am, while encouraging me to grow in grace. I thank you for accepting me like you accepted Peter—as imperfect. Amen.

18

Staying Humble

Our Story

Why should it frighten you that you cannot bear his cross without weakening? On the way to Calvary Jesus fell three times; and you, would you not fall a hundred times, if need be, to prove your love by rising up again with more strength than before your fall?

(Saint Thérèse of Lisieux)

Reflection

Christ had a complete understanding of both his divinity and humanity. In falling on the way to his Crucifixion, he not only showed the human side of his nature, but he allowed others to see it too. Sometimes those of us in ministry find it hard to show our humanity to others. We may feel like we shouldn't (or aren't allowed) to have shortcomings or to make mistakes. That is simply not true.

Some of us may also let our pride get in the way, downplaying or dismissing our shortcomings rather than acknowledging what we can and cannot do. Stress occurs when we develop a superman or superwoman complex, implying we can do anything and everything.

Yet the plain truth is that we are not supermen and superwomen; rather, we are human, and, yes, we too have flaws. We need to claim our humanity and let ourselves off the hook of the often self-imposed requirement that we do everything right and must be everything to everyone. Young people need to know they are cared for and loved, not for what they do, but for who they are—flaws, mistakes, bad decisions, and all. Sometimes we need to remind ourselves of that as well.

Questions to Ponder

- How do I allow myself to make mistakes?
- How do I balance my self-worth with my pride and humility?
- When do I find being humble the most difficult?

For Consideration

- When creating programming and ministry strategies, remember that the goal is good youth ministry, not recognition for yourself.
- Consistently remind yourself of whose work you are doing. (Is it God's or yours?)
- Allow yourself to make mistakes and learn from them; keep a journal of "I wish I had known this before . . ." insights.

Prayer

God of the cross, how hard it must have been for you to fall in front of the jeering crowds. You know what it is like to be humbled. May I learn from your humility and embrace my own. Amen.

19

Dealing with Times of Spiritual Dryness

Our Story

Patiently persevere and do not let yourself get upset. Trust in God, who does not abandon those who seek him with a simple and righteous heart. He will not neglect to give you what you need for your path until he delivers you into that clear, pure light of love. You are meant to receive this great gift, yet it is only through the dark night of the spirit that he will bring you it.

(Saint John of the Cross)

Reflection

Spiritual dryness, according to Saint John of the Cross, is necessary for spiritual and soul growth. In his classic work *Dark Night of the Soul* (Image, 1959), Saint John writes a poem that on the surface may seem like a love poem. However, his explanation of it delivers comfort and challenge to any believer who experiences the dryness or dark night common among us. By going through the dark night, we of course eventually reach the light. When those of us in ministry go through dryness and darkness, the temptation to leave ministry may take hold. When we are authentic and vulnerable, others see us as we really are and can more readily identify with what we are teaching or sharing. Think about the young person who feels confident in his or her beliefs and then experiences tragedy. Our hope is that he or she turns to, not away from, Christ and the Church community during the trying times. As we experience our own difficult and stressful times, we too must turn to Christ and to one another. If young people see us as fully human, we may not be so inclined to think we have to be fully divine; instead, we can just be fully ourselves.

Questions to Ponder

- What spiritual dryness have I experienced myself, and how have I handled such times in the past?
- How do I embrace spiritual struggles and stresses in myself and in those I minister with and to?
- Whom are the spiritual masters I turn to in times of dryness?

For Consideration

- Read Saint John of the Cross's poem and its explanation in *Dark Night of the Soul*.
- Be authentic and honest about your own questions and dryness.
- Be persistent in participating in the sacraments; in times of spiritual questioning and dryness, the ritual of the liturgy and the grace of the sacrament of Penance and Reconciliation can be especially comforting.

Prayer

Provider God who gives all I need and cares for me more than I will ever know, walk even more closely with me through times of spiritual dryness. Rain down on me your life-giving drops of love, and let me be nourished like a desert after a storm. May times of dryness lead me even closer to you. Amen.

20
Taking Time for Prayer

Our Story

> The greatest gift of centered and surrendered people is that they know themselves as part of a larger history, a larger self. . . . People who have learned to live from their center know which boundaries are worth maintaining and which can be surrendered. Both reflect an obedience. If you want a litmus test for truly centered people, that's it: They are always free to obey reality, to respond to what is.
>
> (Richard Rohr)

Reflection

Jesus was very busy. Many people needed his attention, yet he always made time to pray and to be in relationship with his Father. He set an important example for his disciples to follow. Those of us in ministry also have busy and stressful lives, and too often it seems that there is never enough time to do everything we want. The truth is that there is no way to create more time, so we really must think in terms of *taking* time. In order to be Christ-centered people, we must pray. Taking time to pray is just like taking time to eat, sleep, or exercise; we may need to schedule it on a calendar like an appointment or build it into some other daily ritual. We'll never find the time to pray if we don't make it a priority and then *take* the time to do it.

Questions to Ponder

- When is my structured prayer time? If I do not have a structured time, why not?
- What communal prayer experiences, aside from Sunday liturgy, do I participate in?
- How might I incorporate a prayer routine into my daily schedule?

For Consideration

- Seek out resources to help you pray more consistently, and also allow time for spontaneous prayer and for quiet time to listen to God.
- Consider getting a prayer partner. Even if you don't pray together, you can hold each other accountable for taking the time to pray.
- Create a prayer space in your home or office that is easily accessible for prayer time.

Prayer

God who hears and answers me, I do want to spend time with you alone. I know you want that time too. Help me stay true to the time I have set aside for you, and be with me even when I don't make you my first priority. Like a good friend, you are there and will listen to me, just as I will be here for you and will listen to you. Amen.

Acknowledgments

The scriptural quotations contained herein are from the New Revised Standard Version of the Bible, Catholic Edition. Copyright © 1993 and 1989 by the Division of Christian Education of the National Council of the Churches of Christ in the United States of America. All rights reserved.

The excerpt on page 14 is from *The Road to Daybreak: A Spiritual Journey*, by Henri J. M. Nouwen, as quoted in *Seeds of Hope: A Henri Nouwen Reader*, edited by Robert Durback (New York: Bantam Books, 1989), pages 6–7. Copyright © 1989 by Robert Durback.

The excerpt by Saint John Baptist de La Salle on page 16 is from *Meditations by John Baptist de La Salle*, translated by Richard Arnandez and Augustine Loes (Landover, MD: Christian Brothers Conference, 1994), page 257. Copyright © 1994 by the Christian Brothers Conference.

The excerpt by Pope John Paul II on page 30 is from "Meeting with the Priests of the United States of America: Address of His Holiness John Paul II," number 3, at *www.vatican.va/holy_father/john_paul_ii/speeches/1987/september/documents/hf_jp-ii_spe_19870910_sacerdoti-miami_en.html*, accessed December 14, 2006.

The excerpt by Mother Teresa on page 32 is from *Life in the Spirit: Reflections, Meditations, Prayers, Mother Teresa of Calcutta*, edited by Kathryn Spink (New York: Harper and Row Publishers, 1983), page 45. Copyright © 1983 by Kathryn Spink.

The excerpt on page 36 is from *Renewing the Vision: A Framework for Catholic Youth Ministry*, by the United States Conference of Catholic Bishops (USCCB) (Washington, DC: USCCB, Inc., 1997), page 20. Copyright © 1997 by the USCCB, Inc.

The excerpt by Saint Thomas Aquinas on page 40 is found at *www.quotationspage.com/quotes/Saint_Thomas_Aquinas*, accessed December 14, 2006.

The excerpt by Edith Stein on page 42 is from *Edith Stein: Essential Writings*, selected and with an introduction by John Sullivan, OCD (New York: Orbis Books, 2002), page 62. Copyright © 2002 by the Washington Province of Discalced Carmelites, Inc.

The excerpt on page 44 is from *National Directory for Catechesis*, by the USCCB (Washington, DC: USCCB, Inc., 2005), page 186. Copyright © 2005 by the USCCB, Inc.

The excerpt on page 48 is from *Peace of Heart in All Things: Meditations for Each Day of the Year*, by Brother Roger of Taizé (Chicago: GIA Publications, 2004), page 62. Third French edition copyright © 2004 by Ateliers et Presses de Taizé; English translation copyright © 2004 by Ateliers et Presses de Taizé.

The excerpt by Saint Thérése of Lisieux on page 52 is from *A Retreat with Thérése of Lisieux: Loving Your Way into Holiness*, by Elizabeth Ruth Obbard (Cincinnati: St. Anthony Messenger Press, 1996), page 46. Copyright © 1996 by Elizabeth Ruth Obbard.

The excerpt by Saint John of the Cross on page 54 is from *Dark Night of the Soul: Saint John of the Cross,* new translation and introduction by Mirabai Starr (New York: Riverhead Books, 2002), page 68. Translation copyright © 2002 by Mirabai Starr.

The excerpt on page 56 is from *Radical Grace: Daily Meditations*, by Richard Rohr (Cincinnati: St. Anthony Messenger Press, 1995), page 265. Copyright © 1995 by Richard Rohr and John Bookster Feister.

To view copyright terms and conditions for Internet materials cited here, log on to the home pages for the referenced Web sites.

During this book's preparation, all citations, facts, figures, names, addresses, telephone numbers, Internet URLs, and other pieces of information cited within were verified for accuracy. The authors and Saint Mary's Press staff have made every attempt to reference current and valid sources, but we cannot guarantee the content of any source, and we are not responsible for any changes that may have occurred since our verification. If you find an error in, or have a question or concern about, any of the information or sources listed within, please contact Saint Mary's Press.